Harrison Moore

CREDIT REPAIR

SECRETS

Learn how to Restore, Repair and Improve your Credit Report and Protect Yourself from Creditors and Banks using Federal Laws

Copyright © 2020 publishing.

All rights reserved.

Author: Harrison Moore

No part of this publication may be reproduced, distributed or transmitted in any form or by any means, including photocopying recording or other electronic or mechanical methods or by any information storage and retrieval system without the prior written permission of the publisher, except in the case of brief quotation embodies in critical reviews and certain other non-commercial uses permitted by copyright law.

Table of Contents

Introduction 5
Chapter One 8
    What Does Credit Repair Mean? 8
    Can I repair my credit myself, or do I need to hire a company to do it for me? 11
    What is the Credit Repair Organizations Act? 12
    What Is FICO Score and Why Does It Matter? 19
    How to Fix Your Credit Yourself 24
    Improve Your Credit Regardless! 44
    How To Dispute Your Credit Report Errors 50
Chapter Two 55
    How Much Do Credit Repair Services Really Cost 55
    Just the FAQ's on Credit Repair Services 59
    How Credit Repair Company Work 63
    Why Credit Repair Companies Are Necessary 75
    How to Find The Particular Best Credit Repair Company . 78
    Should I Hire a Credit Repair Company to Repair My Credit Or Should I Do it Myself? 83
    Choose the Best Credit Repair Service for You 87
    The Growth Of The Credit Repair Business Opportunity .. 90
Chapter Three 99
    Credit Repair Scams and How to Avoid Them 99
    The Solution to Post-Bankruptcy Bad Credit 103

What Everyone With Bad Credit Should Know About Credit Repair Services 106

Improve Your Credit Score - Credit Repair Companies Put To The Test 112

Fixing Your Finances With Credit Repair 116

Section 609 Credit Repair Method 119

Using Section 609 of the FCRA to Restore NOT Repair Credit 138

Chapter Four 142

Credit Repair After Foreclosure 142

Fast Credit Repair - How To Raise Your Credit Score In 30 Days 145

Exactly How to Rebuild Credit After Bankruptcy 148

Conclusion 151

Introduction

Credit repair is a term that is utilized to allude to the procedure/methods taken or applied so as to transform an awful credit report into a decent one. This repair procedure, otherwise called restoration, should be possible by erasing negative/wrong data from one's record and finding a way to change one's costs so as to raise one's score. The demonstration itself is otherwise called fixing one's credit.

The motivation behind restoration is basic - it is done so as to keep and maintain a decent monetary life without awful evaluating and to such an extent that it will be anything but difficult to move toward budgetary foundations for loans such that one will be affirmed. In any case, it doesn't end there.

A second reason for restoration or fixing is to improve one's chances of getting good financing costs on loans with the end goal that it will be simpler to reimburse over the long haul.

In any case, the need to fix or repair one's document and increment the score is additionally ensuing on different components. These incorporate the need to find a new line of work, advancement, or to carry on with a more joyful life. For example, the number of bosses who presently utilize the record as a device for deciding how qualified a new position candidate is continually expanding every day. In a similar vein, a few bosses likewise utilize their representatives' reports as an appraisal instrument when thinking about advancing some staff in an association.

Taking a gander at these reasons, it turns out to be progressively obvious that there's no avoiding fixing/repairing a terrible record so as to endure the day by day battles individuals will undoubtedly involvement in accounts, especially when making long haul arrangements for a home loan or school reserves.

To reestablish an awful report, all you need do is to contract a specialist credit repair organization to do it for you, or basically do-it-without anyone's help. The do-it-without anyone else's help strategy is getting more grasped by individuals, particularly the individuals who have sufficient opportunity to experience all the procedures in question. In any case, this is best finished with the guide of a restoration-kit/manual. Continuously guarantee you get an ongoing duplicate of your 3-in-1 document before you begin fixing.

Chapter One

What Does Credit Repair Mean?

Great inquiry! It's the basic procedure of "fixing" one's credit by utilizing the accessible buyer credit laws to encourage the evacuation of negative things. The law most much of the time utilized (and referred to) is the Fair Credit Reporting Act (typically called the FCRA) and the entirety of the corrections and modifications made to this law throughout the most recent a very long while. (practically restrictive for the CONSUMER... which is a decent thing..:-)

Is credit repair lawful?

Totally. What's more, the law above promises it also. The straightforward truth is that while there are numerous deceitful individuals on BOTH sides of the credit fence (loan specialists, sellers, and repair offices the same), the key option to challenge, contest and REMOVE things from your report is 100% lawful, genuine or more board for sure!

For what reason does the credit fix business have such an awful name?

Reality? Since there is such a lot of cash on ALL sides. What's more, since credit is such a significant product from numerous points of view... that pioneering individuals of various kinds and stripes have searched out to exploit the credit tested. This incorporates savage lenders as well as credit repair "centers" that frequently guarantee to "fix" your credit medium-term, utilizing techniques that are sketchy, best case scenario... out and out illicit at the very least.

Is credit restoration even conceivable?

Indeed, beyond a shadow of a doubt. Truly, I've actually utilized an assortment of basic, extremely direct, and effective credit repair techniques on my own reports on MORE than one event. (also, giving myself "A" credit in under 4 months, when it began as a "D"... or then again even an "F" time and again) The credit laws are set up, in all honesty, to FAVOR you and me, and beyond a shadow of a doubt, presently is the absolute best time to figure out how to fix your credit after all other options have been exhausted!

Can I repair my credit myself, or do I need to hire a company to do it for me?

Great question - and you can ABSOLUTELY fix your credit yourself. No company is required, although arguably, those who have more professional experience may, in fact, be able to help you get better results faster SIMPLY because they have already learned the landscape (not much different than a plumber can fix your pipes faster than you may!)

What is the Credit Repair Organizations Act?

Are you considering enlisting a credit repair facility yet only somewhat reluctant about your privileges, your cash and

What chance that anything they can accomplish for you all things considered?

Think about what! You are not the only one. Credit repair is a huge business. What's more, there are numerous trustworthy, dedicated assistance experts who fastidiously and determinedly will work to assist you with expelling negative things from your credit record. Obviously, in the notorious yin and yang that our radiant free undertaking economy brings to the table, there are additionally PLENTY of fleeting, corrupt, ill-equipped, and out and out obscure administrators with a bad reputation that will take your cash and not do a thing for you.

Hence, congress enacted the Credit Repair Organizations Act to guarantee there was an unmistakable, reasonable, and handily intervened set of rules that illuminate, in genuinely explicit detail, what a credit repair organization can, and can't do to get your business. It additionally explains how they may charge you (no longer forthright), what sort of terms they can stipulate, and how and when you may demand a discount on the occasion, you would prefer not to seek after the procedure after welcoming them on.

While many credit repair firms have endeavored to go around a portion of the numerous arrangements in the law, and the understandings set out by the Federal Trade Commission on its application, the bottom line is you are MUCH.

More secure today than you were 10 or 12 years back on the off chance that you need your FICO to score kneaded to improve things. Most firms won't chance a protest and strive to guarantee they are giving you the administration and stipends the law orders. It is additionally imperative to recollect that credit repair is splendidly lawful. By excellence of there existing a law that polices the business, you ought to likewise comprehend that by definition, that should crush those naysayer's including some credit department writing) that will propose that reestablishing your credit by employing an expert firm is disagreeable, or far more detestable - ILLEGAL! It most unquestionably isn't don't as well, stress - countless individuals like you and I have profited incomprehensibly from holding their administrations. A couple of rotten ones can ruin the bundle - however, do your due perseverance, comprehend your privileges, and the vast majority of all - get that credit score fixed and do it soon! Life is unreasonably short for awful credit. Stop! They are LYING their backside's off about YOUR credit score!

What is the Importance of the Credit Repair Organizations Act?

Anyone who is looking for the administrations of a credit repair organization is qualified for some fundamental rights. Regardless, the administrators of these administrations ought not to request any installments until and except if the administrations guaranteed have been rendered. The Credit Repair Organization Act (CROA) is sure about what comprises assistance most definitely. The Act likewise plainly expresses the segments of a legitimately restricting contract.

If the conditions set on the contracts are not regarded, at that point, no installments ought to be made. Clients can cancel the contract singularly with no punishment being forced on them. This is the most impressive arrangement of the Credit Repair Organization Act, undoubtedly. He should, in this manner, utilize it each time the contract gives off an impression of being a formula for a super million trick.

The Act stipulates that it is your entitlement to be given the fundamental reports that are going to upgrade your comprehension of the law. The contract should be carefully recorded as a hard copy with the goal that it is acceptable in an official courtroom should you have any lawful concerns later on.

The Act additionally depicts in incredible detail what your privileges and commitments are as a customer of credit revamping administrations. For the shopper to be ensured by the Act, he needs to focus on each statement in the Act. This may here, and there be incomprehensible, attributable to the fact that not all individuals who counsel credit modifying organizations are specialists. Right now, Act gives a decent establishment to you to counsel the administrations of legal counselors at whatever point this is important.

The CROA likewise denies organizations from intentionally giving data that is misdirecting, off base, or bogus. This empowers customers to get equity when they are cheated into marking an outrageous contract. As indicated by the Act, each organization must give all the fundamental contact data in the contract. This data ought to be right. A nitty gritty depiction of the considerable number of administrations that the customer needs to be rendered and the period inside which this will be accomplished ought to likewise be remembered for the contract.

Last Tip: The initial step to get your credit report fixed and your scoring improved is getting a credit report from a standout amongst other Credit Reporting Services in the market. For the most part, since it'll show your credit scores and credit repair organizations request it on all occasions, exploit the free preliminary offers and less expensive costs offered, this permits you to check it more than once every year your rating and credit documents. When you get your credit report, take as much time as necessary to locate a respectable credit repair organization.

What Is FICO Score and Why Does It Matter?

FICO is actually the name of a firm (it's an abbreviation; the firm was formerly called the Fair, Isaac Company, started by a designer, Bill Fair and also a math wizard, Earl Isaac. FICO is a company which concentrates on credit history and other analytics for monetary solutions suppliers. Consequently, consumer credit ratings are typically referred to as FICO scores, also when ratings are actually supplied to customers or potential lenders by an additional entity.

FICO has its own proprietary formula for computing credit scores, although it is recognized that payment past history, length of credit past history as well as credit application are all elements which go into calculating this rating. Also reduced of a score as well as you may find it all yet impossible to acquire a car loan of any type of kind; or at the very least, any kind of financing you'll be supplied will certainly be on remarkably unfavorable terms, specifically in regards to passion rates.

When making a decision whether or not you're a appropriate risk, prospective lenders look at your rating. A greater score implies that lending institutions will certainly view you as extra most likely to repay loans promptly as well as in full; simply puts, they'll assess you as a lesser risk.

Your FICO score is expressed as a 3 figure number which may vary anywhere from 500 to 850. A breakdown of these number ranges as well as what they mean follows:

720-850: This is the highest feasible FICO score array; if your credit score falls under this wide range, you'll normally have a simple time receiving a home loan or various other car loans and also will get one of the most beneficial rates of interest as well as other terms and conditions.

700-719: Dropping simply below the 720-850 wide range will certainly still allow you to obtain financing effortlessly and also you'll additionally have the ability to get beneficial terms and conditions on mortgage as well as other kinds of customer funding.

675-699: This is what is typically related to as suitable credit. You'll likely have the ability to get a loan, although you will not obtain terms and conditions which are as favorable as those you would certainly obtain if your credit score was in the 700-719 or 720-850 varieties.

620-674: If your FICO score is in the 620-674 wide range, you'll probably have difficulty getting excellent terms on a loan; and some lenders could determine that you're as well much of a credit risk to extend funding to in any way.

560-619: Customers with credit ratings between 500 as well as 619 will usually have problem acquiring credit as well as will normally pay substantially higher interest prices than will certainly folks with higher FICO scores.

500-559: If your credit score is in the 500-559 wide range, it's not likely that you'll be able to obtain any type of kind of funding; rather, your priority must be to repair your credit score to make sure that you can certify for a home loan or various other funding in the future.

If you're seeking to improve or maintain your FICO score, it is essential to recognize more about just how your score is determined. The following 5 categories are known to be component of the formula used for computing credit ratings, detailed in order of relevance:

- Payment Past history - 35 %.
- Quantity of Financial obligation - 30 %.

- Length of Credit report - 15 %.
- New Credit - 10 %. Types of Credit - 10 %.

FIX CREDIT EXPRESS is certified and bonded credit consultants to resolve financial challenges that hinder your credit goals. Credit profile improvements are essential efforts to enable you to have better choices in life. Our credit education services remove negative items off credit reports, while providing free credit education with membership to empower your leverage. We raise credit scores by working legally and ethically with you, your financial institutions and the credit bureaus to eliminate unfavorable things and errors from your credit report and include positives.

Our advanced software program system allows us to successfully manage your account while utilizing our expertise to establish an action strategy for your time constraints as well as goal.

How to Fix Your Credit Yourself

You can pay a credit repair company to repair your credit, but if you're willing to take a position some time rather than your cash, then you'll roll in the hay yourself without having to pay knowledgeable. The sole questions you would like to understand before you start are what proportion some time is worth to you, and the way comfortable you're with initiating and managing multiple credit profile related contacts via phone and email. You'll also get to be satisfied with reading and writing quasi-legal documents. You'll find example correspondence online, which may assist you with this.

Step 1: Obtain Your Credit Reports

Your credit score is predicated on a mixture of things and knowledge which is reported about you by 3rd parties to the three major credit reporting agencies. The leading agencies we are concerned with are Experian, Equifax, and TransUnion. These three companies are those who are liable for publishing information about you onto your credit report. However, they're not those responsible for generating knowledge. A creditor, a set agency, or another company (known as data furnishers) will tell Experian, Equifax, and TransUnion what to publish about you, and then the credit bureaus will publish it. They are doing not perform a radical investigation into the legitimacy of the knowledge once they initially report it. Only it's discovered and disputed by you'll it's investigated, at which point it's going to are damaging your credit for months or years. It's also quite common for information to vary on each of your three credit reports, which is like playing Russian roulette whenever your credit pulled if you do not fix all three at an equivalent time. The rationale is because you never know which report your potential landlord, employer, or loan provider goes to tug. Let me offer you an example:

You have never checked your credit reports or felt the necessity to try to do so, however, two years ago, a MasterCard account was fraudulently opened in your name, maxed out, and never paid on. You've got never heard anything about it. The MasterCard company, which defrauded, only reports payment information to Equifax and TransUnion, to not Experian. You've got previously approved for an automobile loan from your bank about nine months ago, so you assume your score is sweet. However, you're turned down within the final stages of your employment application and receive a form within the mail stating that a consumer report utilized in the adverse determination of your employment application. Meaning that albeit your bank pulled your Experian information to verify your creditworthiness for your automobile loan, your potential employer used Equifax or TransUnion and assumed the fraudulent negative MasterCard entry was valid.

Situations almost like the above are quite every day, and whether you're turned down for a loan, a MasterCard application, employment, or an apartment, it's an enormous disruption to your plans and maybe a stress-inducing severe event. Go and check your credit reports immediately, then once a month from here on call to nip this potential problem within the bud.

The first step to require is to quickly obtain a credit report from each of the agencies above. Legally you're allowed to try to do this for free of charge once per annum, and also whenever you're denied credit or suffer another adverse qualifying event supported the results of a consumer report. To urge your free reports, attend annualcreditreport.com, and follow the instructions to get your report. This is often the official government website for obtaining your free credit reports, and it doesn't require a MasterCard or any quite subscription or trial. Some people aren't ready to receive their reports from annualcreditreport.com, thanks to problems verifying their identity or other reasons. If you're unable to get your reports from annualcreditreport.com, you'll either search online for credit report providers; otherwise, you can contact the credit bureaus directly yourself. Typically you'll find providers online, which can charge you $1 for your first month of access to your credit reports and a credit monitoring service, with the cost rising to about $30 per month after that. Remember, it's free for you if you'll get your reports from annualcreditreport.com, so that is undoubtedly your first choice. If you cannot get them there, try a paid provider or contact the bureaus directly either online or by mail and persuade them to supply you with a replica of your report. I always send mail certified, signature required, with a tracking number - and that I highly advise you are doing an equivalent. Keeping an in-depth record of all of your communications with each entity you'll be contacting is of the utmost importance to your success. The dates of your mailings and of the correspondence you receive as a result are significant. Below are the online addresses for the credit bureaus - search their site or search online for instructions for requesting access to your credit report if you're unable to try to do so through annualcreditreport.com.

So, just to be clear:

annualcreditreport.com - official site for obtaining your credit reports - go here first

Experian.com - Equifax.com - TransUnion.com; contact directly if needed

OK, I've received my credit reports within the mail, or I've accessed them online - now what?

Step 2: Reviewing Your Credit Reports for Accuracy

Once you receive your reports, you'll get to review them for accuracy. Check all carefully. There are several sections you'll get to review, and every one contains important information about you, which of them are going to be checked by employers, landlords, utility companies, your telephone provider, and in fact, potential creditors et al. Credit reports from the three agencies each look slightly different, but are generally composed of sections almost like these:

Personal Profile: This section contains your personal information, like your legal name, your current and former addresses, your employment history, and your birth date.

Credit Summary: A snapshot of your credit, including what percentage accounts are opened in your name and their total balance. Reported delinquencies are going to be listed here also.

Public Records: the chances are that you merely likely do not have any public records listed on your report, but they're quite common. Mistakes during this area of your report also are reasonably common and wish to be disputed immediately. This sort of data includes bankruptcy, tax lien, court records, judgments, and support payment.

Credit Inquiries: Any company you've got permitted to review your credit file (called a robust inquiry) are going to be listed here for two years. Quite 3 questions listed during this section can lower your credit score. If you see companies listed during this section that you simply haven't authorized to tug your credit, then they have to be removed. If you check your credit (such as through a paid provider or credit monitoring service like referenced above), your credit score won't be affected. This sort of inquiry understood as a soft inquiry. Typical listings during this section include lenders, and potential or former employers and landlords.

Account History: this is often the precise account information for all accounts opened in your name, which reported to a credit reporting agency. This information is usually positive or negative and collectively has the most critical impact on your credit rating. An outsized amount of inaccurate information often found on some people's credit reports during this section. Positive information reported about you'll remain on your report indefinitely, while contrary information will stay for 7 - 10 years from the date that the account closed, or the time you last made a payment on or acknowledged the alleged debt.

The contact information for all the businesses who are listing information about you'll even be found during this section. These addresses are where you'll be sending your dispute letters if you select to mail them versus filing online (recommended).

The above sections will comprise the bulk of your credit reports. As stated before, undergo them very carefully. Pay special attention to the alleged amounts that you simply owe, the payment dates, and, therefore, the names of the businesses which are reporting the negative information. Note of whether or not it's the first creditor or a debt collector as this may have an impact on the wording of the letters you'll be sending out, an appearance at the account creation dates. In short, undergo and verify that every single data point which is being reported about you thereon credit report is accurate. Make notations of what you think to be incorrect, reconcile this information together with your records, and if it's not precisely the same, then it's going to be being misreported and hurting your credit profile.

Step 3: First Contact

Now that you simply have reviewed your credit reports, the fun part starts. You would like to require all of the knowledge which you would like to be faraway from your report and start writing letters to deal with those issues. You'll put multiple issues on each note. However, I never send quite three points per letter to any agency and that I recommend you do not either. You'll want to send a message to every of the credit bureaus, which details explicitly the explanations the knowledge should be faraway from your report. If it's inaccurate in any way, then legally it must be faraway from your report. Carefully word your dispute letter with diplomatic and professional language, and inform the credit reporting agencies that you simply want them to research the points you raise in your message as you're disputing their accuracy. If you've got evidence supporting your claim, submit a replica together with your dispute letters. The credit agencies want to report correct information, and that they will check out the evidence you send to them. Confirm you are doing not acknowledge that the debt is yours or make any payment offers as this might potentially restart the seven-year clock that the debt is going to reported about you.

After you've got disputed your items, the credit agencies are allowed a minimum of 30 days to reply under the Fair Credit Reporting Act (FCRA). During this point, they're going to contact the info furnisher and plan to verify the accuracy of the debt they're reporting about you. Generally, the info furnisher will simply respond that the info is correct, and zip will change. The agency will send you a letter explaining that they reviewed your claim, and therefore the information was reported to be accurate, and thus they're going to still say it. If you've got submitted proper documentation supporting your position, the agency will review it. However, they'll always side with the info furnisher and refuse to get rid of the wrong items(s) from your report.

If this happens, you will need to contact the original creditors and the collections agencies if they are involved and request validation of the debt they are reporting about you. Typically you will receive some sort of report generated by them, which simply states that they a certain amount of money. This amount will rarely correlate with what you think you owe, or what is being reported onto your credit report. Depending on what type of information you receive from the data furnisher directly, you may be able to simply write a new letter to the credit bureau with copies of the information you received from the data furnisher and an explanation of how the information doesn't correlate with what is being reported on your credit report. They are also required to be able to validate your debt. This is different than verifying it, which is what data furnishers sometimes do. Look up this distinction online and then check to make sure that they have provided the evidence legally required of them to continue reporting information about you.

The parties you will be contacting include:

The three major credit bureaus

Experian

Equifax

TransUnion

The data furnishers

Original creditors

Collection agencies

Attorneys

Others various parties

Dealing with each of these contacts and correctly generating effective correspondence to them, along with corroborating evidence, will be the best and fastest way to fix your credit reports.

Do not enter into any payment negotiations with collections agencies or any other data furnishers without express written statements from them that they will be deleting the "tradeline" once you have fulfilled your payments. This is a very important step when dealing with data furnishers, and forgetting to specify this could cause negative information to stay on your report for much longer in the form of a paid collections account.

Step 4: Raising or Establishing Your Credit Worthiness

If everything looks good on your credit reports and your score still isn't as high as you think it should be, or if you are just new to obtaining credit, there are several things you should be aware of.

Some credit scoring models will give you a lower score for credit card limits or loans, which are under $2,000 - get a limit at least this high if you can.

The average age of all of your combined accounts is important - the older, the better. What this means is that if you have 10 accounts with an average age of 22 years and then you go out and open 4 new accounts to try and raise your score, the average age of your accounts will drop to just under 15 1/2 years old. This will have a negative effect on your credit score and may offset any benefit of opening 4 new accounts, which will also generate 4 new hard inquiries, which will also have a negative effect. Make sure you absolutely need credit before applying for it.

Having over twenty accounts in good standing can raise your score. However, the average age of your accounts will generally make more of an impact on your score than the total number of your accounts (see above).

If you have bad credit or no credit - try this out: Pull your credit reports and fix everything on them that you can so that your credit history is as favorable as possible. Save up $200 dollars, and then go to your bank or go online and find a company that offers secured loans and credit cards - these are generally easy to be approved for because the credit limit is the same as the amount which you deposit. In this case, you will deposit $200 to obtain a secured loan; then, you will take the $200 from your loan and open a secured credit card. This way, you will gain two new accounts that are reporting your timely payments to the credit bureaus for the price of one. Also, you aren't really out any money because even though you deposited $200 to obtain a secured credit card and loan, you now have $200 worth of credit at your disposal. Make sure you make timely payments on these two accounts, and your score can easily go up 75 points or more in just a few months. If you can manage a $2,000 secured loan, then you will get the benefit of having a loan and a credit card with credit limits of at least $2,000 each, which will both report to the major credit bureaus and can raise your score even more. If you decide to do this, make sure your secured card provider reports to all three major credit bureaus - and try to pay off your credit card in full each month.

On-time payments to your accounts in good standing are the best way to raise your score and keep it there.

If you are offered a lower credit card limit than you want, you can always call the financial provider and request a higher limit. Sometimes all they need is a little additional information to approve you for thousands of dollars more.

The amount of your credit limit which you actually borrow matters; your debt to credit ratio is what credit agencies use to quickly see how much of your available credit you are using each month. This amount can change on a daily basis and has a major effect on your credit score. Keep the total amount of your debt down to about 20% or less of your available credit to look favorable.

Don't max out individual cards; if you have $10,000 of total credit on three cards of $4,000, $5,000, and $1,000 dollars, don't max out any individual card. Keep each of them at 20% or less utilization to save on interest and to keep your cards from being individually over-utilized.

Keep your cashback by paying your cards in full each month. As long as the accounts are active and being used, paying them off each month won't look bad for your score. By not carrying a monthly balance, you will avoid paying interest completely while still receiving cash back for using your cards. In this case, you can actually make money by properly managing your credit cards if you are disciplined.

Paying twice can save you thousands; many loans can be paid off much quicker by simply taking the monthly amount owed, splitting it in two, and paying it off in two separate payments each billing cycle. If you can add just a little extra in each payment, your savings could be significant, and it could speed up the time it takes to pay off your loan by months. Mortgages and car loans are great for this strategy.

Improve Your Credit Regardless!

At one time, many, numerous years prior, you could experience existence secretly your personality, your credit history, your open records, or having individuals keeping an eye on your life.

Not all that today!

Appears just as today, everybody realizes all they have to think about you: your personality, your credit history, your open records, or the individuals making requests about you. This would all be able to be accredited to PCs, the web, and the "advanced world" we live in. What's more, of course.......... Credit Companies!

Did you realize your credit score and obligation picture all assume significant jobs in accomplishing your money related objectives? Your credit score and obligation picture really have an influence in the entirety of the accompanying:

Moneylenders may utilize your credit score for advance choices and terms in advance. The advanced the credit score, the lower the financing cost.

Home loan organizations may utilize your credit score to choose whether or not you can get an advance and the financing costs they set.

Insurance agencies can choose whether or not you get protection and the rates that concern you.

Proprietors may utilize your credit score to decide if they lease to you, the lease they charge, and the security store the request.

Credit card organizations may utilize your credit score to acknowledge or decrease your application and furthermore decide the loan fee.

So you can undoubtedly observe why with a sound score and capable past credit conduct, you will make it more probable for moneylenders to offer you lower financing costs on the things we referenced above and a lot more preferences that favor you. Knowing your score and how it looks at along these lines turns out to be significant!

Much increasingly significant is:

- Knowing the data and steps you need by and by to address your credit report.
- Realizing where to go and what to do to improve your credit score.
- Realizing how to address your credit score in as quick a period conceivable.
- Realizing how to expel negative things from your credit report.
- Realizing how to depend on yourself as opposed to another person to repair your credit score

You might be thinking, "why not employ somebody to repair my credit report?" Or, "why not go straightforwardly to the credit authorities?" Or, "why not simply let time fix my credit report?" Or "exactly what amount of distinction can my credit make?"

Credit Repair Services may sound fascinating, yet in reality, they might be substantially more difficult than they are worth. They may intentionally haul out their administrations to charge you more. Additionally, in light of the structures you should acquire and round out are muddled, you may very well also have done it without anyone's help.

Books to incorporate printed books, digital books, or sound projects; may likewise solid tempting, yet even the best of them expect you to work your own letters and make sense of for yourself how to best question negative things. Likewise, exceptionally confused!

Credit Bureau Instructions may likewise appear to be luring. However, they could be equivalent to "the wolf educating the sheep!" They might be free, yet you get what you pay for! "Purchaser, Beware!"

One of your objectives ought to be to discover and recognize a program that will help you in Repairing You Credit Score!

The chance that you are searching for a total downloaded PC program for credit repair search for one, which tells you the best way to do it without anyone else's help. Simply be certain they offer:

1. Basic, quick, and compelling methods for improving your credit score.

2. Genuine point and snap effortlessness without any letters to compose, no laws to comprehend, without any entanglements at all.

3. Customization of letters, effectively composed particularly for you with answers to credit agencies in a basic productive way.

4. Quick track "strategies" that can really deliver brings about only days.

5. A computerized contest tracker program customized for your necessities.

6. A "self-coordinated" framework that permits you to invest less energy than you would on the off chance that you paid for help or a lawyer.

Projects can be found on our site. To become familiar with credit repair, follow our connection to the area on Legal, and you will be satisfied to gain proficiency with the means important to repair your credit score.

How To Dispute Your Credit Report Errors

Your credit report contains significant data about you. It, for the most part, incorporates facts about your distinguishing proof information, your bill-paying propensities, requests, and open record data.

Credit departments incorporate and offer your credit data to organizations, which use it to assess your credit applications. In this way, it is significant that your credit report contains total and precise data.

Under the Fair Credit Reporting Act, you reserve the options to dispute the culmination and exactness of data in your credit records.

On the off chance that you discover data in your credit record that you accept is incorrect; what you have to do is to finish the uncommon examination demand structure that accompanies your credit report. Adhere to the structure's directions to round out all of the fundamental data.

You may likewise need to append a letter to your finished structure, dated and marked by you, and alongside duplicates of any documentation you have that demonstrates the blunder in your credit report.

The documentation may incorporate duplicates of dropped checks, deals receipts, account proclamations, or past correspondence among you and the creditor in question.

Joining a letter to the examination demand structure is constantly a smart thought on the off chance that you don't believe that the credit agency's examination structure gives you enough space to clarify why you think there is a mistake in your report.

Keep a duplicate of your finished examination demand structure, letter, and reinforcement documentation. They give you the records of what you said and when you said it. Likewise, the date of the letter will tell you when you ought to have heard back from the credit departments.

When you have finished the examination demand structure, mail it, alongside your letter, and duplicates of any documentation. Send it by confirmed mail with a solicitation for an arrival receipt. At the point when you recover the marked receipt, document it with the remainder of your credit record data.

At the point when a credit agency gets a dispute, it must research and record the ebb and flow status of the disputed things inside a "sensible timeframe," - somewhere in the range of 30 and 45 days, except if it accepts the dispute is "unimportant or unessential."

With that, the credit department can't confirm a disputed thing, and it must erase it.

On the off chance that your report contains mistaken data, the credit authority must address it.

In the event that a thing is deficient, the credit department must finish it.

On the off chance that an examination doesn't resolve your dispute, the Fair Credit Reporting Act grants you to record an announcement of up to 100 words to clarify your side of the story.

The credit department must remember this clarification for your credit report each time it sends it out. Credit agency workers frequently are accessible to assist you with the wording of your announcement.

Know, in any case, that when negative data in your report is exact, just the progression of time can guarantee its evacuation.

Credit agencies are allowed by law to report liquidations for a long time and other negative data for a long time.

Likewise, any negative data might be accounted for uncertainly for use in the assessment of your application form:

- $50,000 or more in credit;

- an extra security arrangement with a face measure of $50,000 or more;

- thought for a vocation paying $20,000 or more.

Chapter Two

How Much Do Credit Repair Services Really Cost

In the desperation to repair their credits as soon as possible, often people avail credit repair services from different companies around the world. By this, they get the advantage of saving time and also utilizing the experience of the professionals of the service providing company.

However, availing such services is almost equivalent to outsourcing the tedious task of legal application for removal of inaccurate entries from your credit account and paying them for the same. Thus, these services are kind of expensive compared to the costs incurred if one undertakes all the procedures on his own.

Lexington law is the most famous and trusted credit Repair Company of all time till date. It has all sorts of schemes that let you increase your credit score 50, 100 or

200 points. Moreover, all the proceedings of this company are completely legal. It is operated by a group of attorneys. It also helps you forward applications for reporting dispute in your credit accounts.

The cost of credit repair by through Lexington law varies depending upon the kind of task that they are doing for you. To open an operating relationship with the Lexington law, the initial sign up charges are $99. Besides that, in order to avail very basic services and consultancy, the Lexington law charges you $39 as a monthly fee. So the total amount of money you pay depends upon the amount of time your credit repair takes. The Lexington law has the concept of monthly charges. Thus, there is no additional fee for any number of disputes and there are no other hidden costs.

For availing some of the premium services offered at Lexington law, the charges are obviously different. There are "Concord programs" that promise you improved results and a faster credit repair. It requires an additional $20 per month to avail the "Concord Standard" service. The concord standard program has features like handling various targeted legal and goodwill interventions, catering to escalated information requests, debt validation in accordance to Fair Debt Collection Practices Act etc.

Another program called the "Concord Premium" provides you with a monthly report on your credit score improvement analysis, in addition to the normal and "Concord Standard" services. It also has features like "Reports Watch (TM)" which is a service that alerts you as soon as it detects any changes in your credit account. This facilitates a close watch on your credit score. "Inquiry Assist (TM)" caters to addressing complex enquiries regarding credit repair. This facility is requires an initial registering fee of $99 with monthly charges of $79.

These are the prices of the most renowned companies in the field of credit repair. It is known for its reliability and legality. Paying this amount takes a huge burden off your shoulders, and your credit score future definitely lies in safe hands. You can however also find other much cheaper or more expensive companies in the market and avail there services. But it is always advised to do thorough research in the background of a company before hiring them.

Just the FAQ's on Credit Repair Services

If you have bad credit and are looking for ways to improve it, you probably have a lot of questions about the best way to get the ball rolling. In this article we'll cover the top frequently asked questions about credit repair and professional credit repair services. By the end of the article you'll have more information you can use to begin repairing your credit.

Q: Isn't it true that you can't change what is on your credit report, so credit repair services can't really do you any good?

A: No, that is a myth. The Fair Credit Reporting Act states that you can contact the credit reporting agencies and dispute negative items on your credit reports. Any information that you feel may be incorrect, misleading, incomplete or unverifiable can be disputed. If the credit bureau cannot verify that the information you are disputing is correct, then it must be deleted from your report. Credit repair services can help you with the process of disputing inaccurate or questionable items.

Q: How much do credit repair services cost?

A: It depends on the company you choose. Most will charge you a one-time set-up fee to review your credit situation. They will then decide whether or not they can help you, and if so, they will prepare a plan of action for cleaning up your credit and usually assign your account to one of their specialists. This fee varies widely among different companies, but is frequently less than $100. Most of them charge a monthly fee (usually $40 to $80 per month, although it may occasionally be more or less) to provide services like dispute assistance, credit monitoring, and credit education. Some even provide identity theft insurance.

Q: Can't I just repair my credit on my own?

A: You can, but it is a time-consuming and often frustrating process. One of the primary benefits of hiring credit repair services is that they save you time. For every item on your credit report that you want to dispute, you must write a letter, send it, monitor the time that has passed (credit agencies only have 30 days to respond), follow up with the bureau if the deadline has passed and so on. If you have a lot of incorrect or unverifiable information on your report, this process can take a substantial portion of time.

Conclusion

Millions of Americans have damaged credit, but with the help of credit repair services, bad credit can usually be improved significantly. The Fair Credit Reporting Act gives consumers the right to challenge incorrect information. Take advantage of that right and investigate your credit report today. A credit repair service can help you dispute incorrect information and save you a great deal of time. If you have bad credit, it's in your best interest to take advantage of the great things credit repair services can offer.

How Credit Repair Company Work

Credit Repair Companies, generally speaking, have gotten a "bad rap" and not without good reason! A lot of scammers have masqueraded as credit repair agencies, promising to help relieve their clients of their credit problems. But in the end, all they have "relieved" them of is their hard-earned money!

But not all credit repair organizations are crooks! There are many reputable credit repair companies that provide a valuable and much needed service to the consumer.

A poor credit score can dig deep into your pockets and drain away your hard-earned money on excessively high interest rates. At the same time, repairing your credit is a time-consuming process, which requires close follow-up and often specialized and customized appeals for removing inaccurate negative data from your credit report.

You are probably aware that there are a huge number of credit repair companies and credit repair lawyers ready to offer their services, but you don't know which one to choose. You may have heard too many stories of people being left with nothing to show for their money, and for that reason, you are very wary and indecisive.

Here are five factors that will help you reach an intelligent and informed decision:

1. Professionalism - is the company you are considering professional? Check out their web site carefully and see whether you are comfortable with what you find there.

- Is the website easily navigable?
- Does it have a page with FAQs that can help guide you?
- Do they have a live chat or fast-response email service to answer your queries?

- Is there counseling offered free by the companies?
- Does it make extraordinary claims? (NOT a good sign!)

Check carefully every aspect, and trust both your logic and your gut feelings.

2. Ethical - it is extremely important that the credit repair companies you choose behaves ethically. Do not fall for agencies that claim they can remove all your negative accounts, whether they are being accurately reported or not. You should expect to remove only those accounts which are being inaccurately reported.

Do not be tempted to avail of illegal means to increase your score. You might be inviting more trouble than you could handle. Check on the Internet for reviews or feedback on the credit repair companies you have chosen. Be on the lookout for any reports of scams. Check whether the company is affiliated with reputed organizations such as the ECRA

(Ethical Credit Repair Alliance) or the BBB (Better Business Bureau) which will ensure that they adhere to strict codes of conduct.

3. 24/7 monitoring - credit repair means much more than just "credit repair." It means counseling, education, awareness, and monitoring among other things. Regular monitoring and immediate intervention when negative remarks find their way into your credit report are far more effective in maintaining a good credit score that just repairing it. Are the credit repair companies offering you more? Do they have these ancillary services on their menu?

4. Reasonable - it is true that credit repair companies are in business to turn a profit. However, this should not be at the cost of their clients. The best business relationships, ones that survives time and changes in technology, are often associated with the offer of value-for-money by companies. You need to feel

happy about the price and services offered. Research these aspects well enough so that you will be empowered to bargain for the best offer. Do not feel shy about negotiating.

5. Offer solutions - you need solutions. The best credit repair companies are those who are able to draw you out and learn about your problems in detail, so that they can work out a customized solution for you as an individual. This is very important because no two financial problems will be alike, and what works fine for one person might not work at all for another. Look for a credit repair agency that is geared toward offering solutions - "tailor made" solutions for YOU!

Many of us hear the term "credit repair services" and automatically think it's a scam. This is because many of them are, and only attempt to steal your money and drip-dry your wallet. However, we'll be taking a look at what an ideal, reputable, efficient, and proven credit Repair Company does. This company assists people in repairing their credit quickly, usually within a couple months. This can take at least a year for a novice to try to do, if they are successful. The most important factor to keep in mind when seeking credit repair services is that it is a marathon, not a sprint. It takes delicate time and resources to repair a credit report, so you need to find a company that is passionate about helping you, and has a proven track record. We will also discuss tips and tricks you can use to ensure you're picking a winning company to help keep yourself and your wallet safe.

Firstly, let's go over safety. This is the main concern when selecting a credit repair company. A good credit repair company doesn't have the words "wire" or anything of the sorts on their site. They proudly accept payment via check, credit, or debit card, just as any legitimate business does. You won't be sending nonrefundable money to them, or making cash deposits into their account. These are the same trusted payment options you use everywhere else, and credit cards are also backed by the credit companies' award winning fraud protection, so you know you're safe. Other companies that claim to want to truly help you, often drip-feed your wallet taking $100 month-by-month, and falling back on the excuse that they never promised anything, but would "try" to do their best for you. As much as it's a fact that nothing can be promised, because ultimately it's up to the credit bureaus, they live on that excuse to suck peoples' wallets dry. A good credit repair company isn't like that, and you're welcome to ask any of their many satisfied customers.

Second, some type of reasoning behind their services is what you're looking for. How can they help you? What are they capable of clearing from your reports? What is the turnaround time? Do they have any examples of their work? These are all great questions to be asking not only the company, but also yourself when sourcing professional credit repair help. A good company separates itself from the fakes out there in a number of ways. They show you a detailed in-depth video of a consumer's credit report. A video would be ideal so you can then note the differences. They go over how their report looked at one point, and also at another point to show the improvements. You want to see a timeframe of around a couple months. They should take time to show you the basics of what they can do for you in order to begin building trust with potential clients.

By now, you're hopefully leaning towards using a good credit repair company for your credit report issues. But how do they work? A good credit repair company works off of government legislature to fairly represent you to the credit reporting bureaus. To ease some of your curiosity, their strategy involves them using, on your behalf, the Fair Credit Billing Act, Fair Credit Reporting Act, and the Fair Debt Collection Practices Act. True knowledge and understanding of all these pieces of legislation gives us the ability and the confidence to legally challenge items in your credit reports. Each one of these acts can be viewed at: www.ftc.gov. You may also be asking how long it takes to see results. Once you receive your credit reports from all 3 credit bureaus, a good credit repair company will aggressively remove the negative debt from your credit report. By law, the credit agencies must respond to your dispute letters within 30 days from the actual dispute claim, and you should definitely see results on your credit file within 30-45 days.

Hopefully, the above paragraph gave you a reasonable idea as to how they operate. They're basically like your lawyers, but to the credit bureaus! Trust them to work with you, and you surely won't be disappointed. If you have any questions, comments, or concerns, reach out! The first step to bettering your financial future is to allow them to help you in combating the intimidating credit bureaus. You could also try to fix your credit report yourself, but when a novice attempts to do that, the credit bureaus log each and every dispute, so this can make it harder later on down the line when you attempt to seek professional help. Let the expert's help you from the get go! It is important that you don't begin contacting the credit bureaus and seeking disputes without knowing what you're doing. This can only hurt you and make you look less serious to them, and they will attempt to take advantage of that. You must convey to them that you mean business, and allowing a professional outfit to represent you is generally the best option available.

So why hire a professional outfit to professionally represent you? It has gotten to the point where almost everything is based on your credit history. With a better and more accurate credit file, you can receive lower credit card and home mortgage interest rates, lower automobile finance charges, lower down payments, lower insurance rates, and more pre-approved credit. Foremost, restoring your credit will give you more peace of mind and will also eliminate certain stress. Therefore you can benefit greatly by taking advantage of professional services. Most of the important things in your life such as your car, job, financial standing, and job, can all be affected by how well your credit report is. If you are in the position where you need credit repair assistance, you need to consult a professional company that specializes in removing derogatory remarks on your accounts, remove accounts that are in collections, and other bad histories within your credit report that can prevent you from obtaining future loans, having to satisfy for higher interest rates, and other obstacles throughout your financial future. You may also want to fix your credit fast in case you need to acquire any new loans for a family emergency, a new vehicle, getting a new job, or even a new home.

Why Credit Repair Companies Are Necessary

Credit has been essential to every person's purchasing capacity. With all the available products you wish to possess, you cannot afford to buy them all. That is the power of credit, making things possible for you. That is why having a good credit is really important. Having a good credit rating means having more opportunities to purchase. And knowing that there are many credit cards available today, all you need is to have a good credit record. The better the credit, the more options can be offered to these people. But the truth is, having a good credit rating is hard to achieve. Especially with many different cards one can maintain, it will be hard for a person to resist the temptation of buying more.

For this reason, we really are in need of credit repair. If you are one of the many people who are in dire need for credit repair, do not worry any longer. There are numerous credit repair companies and they are even available online. Just that is just easy! These services can really help you out. The problem now is deciding what repair service you should choose. However, choosing what repair service depends on how bad your rating is.

For people who really have a large amount of debt, they need specific online credit repair services. You can avail of credit counseling so that you will be guided on what to do with your situation. These credit repair services can help in a few different ways. The first step these credit repair companies do is to work with you and ensure accurate credit report from you. It must be made sure that you always pay attention on your credit rating. This is a very common problem since most creditors do not speak of the real situation. Inaccuracies happen most of the time that is why it is very important to deal with them immediately to prevent more damages on your record. Using secured credit cards with a debt consolidation loan can give valuable insight to help you recover from the pit that you unfortunately fell in. So, the earlier you help yourself, the more chances of faster recovery from a bad credit.

If you can not afford to pay immediately, these companies will just take care of your credit card balance. In worst cases, they will tell their clients to claim bankruptcy. Credit repair companies have saved a large majority of people who suffer from bad credit. If you have bad credit, then search for the best repair service now. It is not too late. You can still do something.

How to Find The Particular Best Credit Repair Company

Some people would actually prefer to work with a credit repair company when compared with go throughout the trouble regarding fixing their credit problems on their own. But exactly how will you know if the company an individual hired is the best credit repair company?

Getting impressed using two or more companies is just typical since most of them give quite tempting purports to their customers. The one line which separates each and every company is the actual intense truthfulness on their claims. And a lot of the time, you might be already around the trap when you find out that you have just vacant promises, poor service that produces low quality results and dishonest practices. How can you tell the sincere offer from the tricking ones? The best credit company will probably be hired using the assistance of the following advice.

Best Credit Repair Company tip #1: Very best Customer Service. Sometimes you should be patient adequate to support your self when controlling the bureaus. Consumers would really welcome someone who could lend them a hand within times when their particular credit isn't on their healthiest level. How well the client service associates answer each of the customer's inquiries is amongst the bases regarding finding the best credit repair business.

Best Credit Repair Company tip #2: Best Track Record. The company overview must be good enough as well as real to impress the customers. Inspect how a company was established and the way long it was in the business. Lawsuits as well as court incidents are parts of the public information so you are able to check if the company is associated with any before. A word of caution on depending on a Better Business Bureau rating; it has ended up discovered that numerous A-rated companies, whom had much more complaints than C rated companies, obtained the higher score because they paid out the Better business bureau big bucks for it. This makes your rating associated with credit businesses to be difficult to rely on.

Best Credit Repair Company idea #3: Fair Company warranty and Cancellations Policy. And they're willing to reimbursement your repayment if ever you are not satisfied with the service these people rendered.

The actual best credit repair company now offers to check the advancement of your credit rating online. Everything that offers something to do with your current interest is installed in the open. Whether you want to monitor your concern or not, they'll provide you the info since that is part of the services they offer.

Here are several of the most picked out services offered by the best credit repair firm:

- Assist with creditors, at the appropriate interval, by mailing Creditor Direct letters
- Send out dispute queries
- Ask for the office to change or even delete any inaccurate info found on the report
- Guide you as you deal with the actual fraudulent activities of a number of collection agencies.
- Guide you in creating your very good image throughout the eyes in the bureaus and also lenders
- Solve your identity theft problem

Truthful along with realistic include the two qualities that best credit repair organization are. The best credit repair business wouldn't promise a person things that will never happen in reality; instead they are going to give you the time where final results can really take place. One cannot compare the length of time they notice progress around the service they acquired via another consumer since enhancement varies on each circumstance.

Should I Hire a Credit Repair Company to Repair My Credit Or Should I Do it Myself?

Should I hire a credit repair company? This is by far one of the most widely asked questions by people who need to fix their credit and get their FICO scores increase. The answer however is not that cut and dry, while some people should hire a company to get the job done most should not and you will find out why in the article below!

Why You Do Not Need a Credit Repair Company

The biggest reason you do not need to hire a company to fix your credit is the simple fact that you can get the exact same results for a lot less money, often a lot faster as well! This is a fact that not many people realize!

First you must understand that these for profit companies are in business for one reason, to make money. They make that money by charging clients a monthly fee. So the longer they can charge you that fee the more they make giving them incentive to take longer then needed!

In most cases, you pay them a $75 set up fee then on average $99 a month. So just doing some basic math shows that for 3 months of credit repair you will be paying $372! Plus what these companies will not tell you is that all letters and correspondence from the bureaus will be sent to you and you will have to mail, or drive it down to them, so it is not really a hands off process for you!

If I Do Not Hire a Company To Fix My FICO Score What Should I Do?

The best way to get your FICO scores increased and your credit report cleaned up is to use a credit repair kit. However not just any of these kits will do, you need to make sure that you buy a the right kit that is going to supply you everything you need to get to work!

What Does a Good Credit Repair Kit Contain?

- A Step By Step Plan To Follow
- Credit Dispute Letter Templates
- A Plan To Rebuild Your Credit History
- Tips To Manage and Pay Down Your Current Debt Levels
- Tips on How To Deal With Creditors
- Bonus Products To Help Yo Get The Most From Your Efforts
- How To Order and Read Your Credit Report

Choose the Best Credit Repair Service for You

When you are looking to hire a company to fix your credit you should know what your goals are. This should be researched just like any other professional that we need and use. I will cover the five areas you want to compare when picking the best credit repair company.

The first thing you want to know is what you are getting with the company. There are many companies out there that simply mail out template dispute letters to the credit bureaus alone. These types of credit repair companies often get you what we refer to as soft deletions. Soft deletions are items which are taken off your credit report in the verification process but end back on your report often in a matter of weeks.

You want a company who disputes with the credit bureaus but who also goes to the source of the problems. The source will be your creditors and collection companies, removing items from the source to ensure they do not just pop back on your report. Correcting the problem at the source will insure that the credit correction is permanent.

Total cost is almost always overlooked by the consumer who is lured in by small monthly payments. The part that they fail to mention is the end date;because it does not exist. Yes the monthly payment may seem appealing at first but when you compare, they often cost more than $1,000 a year. Consumers can also be stuck in this never-ending billing for years with little to no results.

A recent study showed that with only a 50 point increase to their credit score the average consumer would save $400 a month. Now do the total cost on that same low monthly payment service for two years. With a price of $1000 per year, now add in the 24 months of lost savings at $400 a month. The total cost would really be $11,600, scary but true! You always want to choose a credit repair service built for speed, a service that will go after all negative inaccurate information immediately and then on every single round.

The time line in which you can expect your results is a big factor as exposed in the total cost. It has been my experience that when people are looking for credit repair there is generally a major purchase happening or coming soon. The time that you will get your results should be explained but if any service guarantees a specific outcome in an exact time they are violating the law. Find out what the average client has experienced for the success you need to achieve.

Results are the foundation to better credit. If you do not get results then you are just wasting your hard-earned money. When choosing a company you want to see actual results. Any company who is successful should be able to produce real results for you. The real results you want to see are actual credit reports showing the before and after results including the actual responses from the credit bureaus themselves. Client testimonials are also a great resource to explore the best are in video with real people explaining in their own words of what a service has done to help them.

The reputation that a company has can say a lot about their product or service. Credit repair has earned a well deserved black eye because of the deceptive practices of the unethical companies out there. The internet provides you the ability to quickly research the company that you are considering hiring. If they have a bad online reputation, come up on one of the many consumer protection sites, or you cannot find them period you better be very careful.

The Growth Of The Credit Repair Business Opportunity

Everyone is saying that times are hard and that no one is making any money nowadays. But that doesn't mean you have to believe it. Rise above all the negativity about who is earning what (and who isn't earning anything) and do something for yourself. Start a business that has proven to be successful with your own credit repair business.

Why should you start a credit repair business?

Even if you have just recently started looking into what business to start, you probably already realize the advantages of a credit repair business! There are many reasons to consider credit repair.

It is a business that can be run easily at home, with little start up cost required. You can do it from your kitchen table with just your laptop. You can do it as a full-time job or just for a couple of hours each day, and you get to set your own hours.

And, it is a business that can succeed even if the economy is bad.

But many people love being in the credit repair business because it gives them the chance to help people while earning a living. Credit repair may not be the first thing that comes to mind when you are thinking of ways to help people, but it really is!

When a client has a bad credit rating, they may not be able to get the new car they need, or the home of their dreams. Bad credit may mean they can't start a business, or even get a job.

Even worse (and more frustrating), is that sometimes having a bad credit rating isn't even the client's fault! Mistakes can easily happen on a person's credit report; their name or social security number can be mixed up with someone else's.

These errors can be very difficult to correct, and problems from these errors can get even more serious. Your client may not only have problems getting the loan they need for a new car, but they may be getting harassing phone calls from creditors. And, they may end up having their wages garnished. All for something that isn't their fault!

Or maybe your client didn't take their credit very seriously in their younger days, and now they need some help getting their credit report cleaned up. They are anxious to make things right, but they just need a little help figuring out the best way to repair their credit.

This is where you come in as a credit repair professional, where you get to be the hero!

The FTC and members of congress realize credit report errors are a problem

Even the government is concerned about credit report errors and the impact these can have on consumers. According to a Federal Trade Commission (FTC) study of the U.S. credit reporting industry, 5% of consumers had errors on one of their three major credit reports. These errors could lead to them paying more for important things such as auto loans and insurance.

The study also found that:

- One in four consumers identified errors on their credit reports that might affect their credit scores
- One in five consumers had an error that was corrected by a credit reporting agency after it was disputed, on at least one of their three credit reports
- Four out of five consumers who filed disputes experienced some modification to their credit report
- Slightly more than one in 10 consumers saw a change in their credit score after the credit reporting agency modified errors on their credit report

- Approximately one in 20 consumers had a maximum score change of more than 25 points and only one in 250 consumers had a maximum score change of more than 100 points.

Sen. Claire McCaskill (D-Mo.) testified in front of a Senate Commerce Committee at a hearing on inaccurate information on credit reports. She told them, "Errors can mean the difference between obtaining a car loan or not, or paying a higher price for a mortgage. Errors can result in credit issuers, like a small town bank, declining credit to a potentially valuable customer, or issuing credit to a riskier customer than intended."

She suggested that the industry needed financial penalties to keep similar mistakes from happening. Sen. David Rockefeller (D-WV), chairman of the Senate Commerce Committee, also suggested that legislation was needed.

"The credit bureaus have a legal obligation to take all reasonable steps to maximize the possible accuracy of credit reports, and when they do contain errors, provide consumers with the means to fix them," said Rockefeller. "I expect this industry to do everything it can to ensure that the system works for the ones that it impacts the most, everyday Americans. If today's hearing uncovers problems with the credit reporting industry, I urge these companies to tackle those problems with a sense of urgency."

Clearly, consumers need help with this important issue.

How to take advantage of a credit repair business opportunity

The first step to helping your clients, once you decide to be a part of the credit repair business, is to learn all you can about the credit repair business. You need to learn the secrets to credit repair and how to submit credit disputes on behalf of your clients. You need to have a thorough understanding of how credit reports work, so you can help your clients to understand them.

It may sound like too much to take on, especially if you don't consider yourself a financial wizard. However, there are some simple ways that you can get credit repair business training.

- To start with, you can read as much about credit and credit repair as you can. Look around online for credit repair forums and join in on the discussions.
- Get your own credit report and take a close look at it.
- Find a mentor, and someone who has been in the credit repair business for years.

This may not be as easy as it sounds, though. This is where a credit repair business training resource comes in. This is a great way to communicate with professionals who have been in the industry for years. It will also help you to educate yourself about the industry and the best way you can help your clients. It will help you understand what you can and can't do when negotiating with your client's creditors and collection agencies, and it will help you to ensure that your client won't be taken advantage of.

Chapter Three

Credit Repair Scams and How to Avoid Them

Recently my friends at Liberty Mortgage Company sent me an email alert regarding the latest scams in the credit repair market. The mortgage company receives applications every day that have some credit issues that could block the path to home ownership. Many of the people they talk with think that their credit issues are being repaired. Unfortunately, these applicants often have fallen for one of the many credit repair scams that set their traps for well meaning home buyers with a few credit problems.

Mortgage loan qualification requirements are stricter today than in the past - FHA / VA and Conventional Home Loan sources are requiring ever higher FICO scores so the average applicant may need to improve their credit report before they can qualify for a home loan. With the demand for housing beginning to grow, it makes a very ripe market for scammers. Most popular credit repair scams promise to wipe your credit report clean of all negative information. They usually charge an up front fee, sometimes as much as $1,500 for their service. Often all the scammers will do is dispute all the negative information on your credit report. This is something you can do on your own for free.

Another "We will fix it" scam for a fee is to tell you that they will get you a new social security number. The idea is with a new number most credit agencies would have to start a new file under that number with your name and it wouldn't have the negative information that may have been reported under your old SS number. The truth is, the Social Security Administration almost never agrees to assign a new SS number to an individual who already has a file and number. What these "credit repair" scammers are doing is filing with the IRS for an EIN (Employer Identification Number) under your name. It's also a nine-digit number that looks like a social security number, but is actually a number assigned to a business. This number is used by the IRS to identify companies for tax payment purposes.

If you fall for this one, the consequences are far reaching. By using an EIN as your SS number, you change how your income is reported to the IRS. You'll find it's a big problem when you retire and the Social Security Administration has no record of your work history. Not only will your social security checks be in jeopardy, you may find yourself accused of conspiring to commit fraud with possible jail time in your future. Remember, there is no magic formula to repairing your credit score, and no big secrets that only a credit repair company has access to. Credit score repair is actually a fairly simple process of writing letters and then following up, and it can be done by anyone. The scammers are out there, and they want your money so be informed and don't be a victim.

The Solution to Post-Bankruptcy Bad Credit

Doing credit repair after you have had a bankruptcy is probably one of the smartest things you can do for your credit profile. If you believed the story your attorney told you after your bankruptcy that your credit report would take care of itself, you are probably regretting that. No doubt your credit report does not look like you hoped it would after your bankruptcy.

Self credit repair is your solution. Don't be misled by credit repair companies that claim they can get your bankruptcy removed from your report. The fact of the matter is that when you fill out a loan application you will most likely have to declare if you have had a bankruptcy within the last 7 years anyhow. If you don't disclose this, you are committing fraud. You should not commit fraud! It is dangerous.

So, your bankruptcy is discharged and your credit report still looks like a mess. You still have accounts that show up with balances on them when they were included in your bankruptcy and should show no balance. Other accounts show a balance of zero, but they still have a negative rating on them. You are probably in a situation where you pretty much need to dispute anything that is negative on your credit report. You have the right to dispute anything you don't feel is reporting 100% accurately because you have the right to have everything on your report be 100% accurate. That is the law found in the Fair Credit Reporting Act.

You should already have a copy of your credit report. You can get this online or you can probably get it from the lender that denied your credit. Just ask them for it. They can usually scan it and email it to you as a PDF file. Once you have your report, read it and decide what you think you need to dispute. This can be a bit of a daunting task, especially if you don't really know how to read the report. If you got your report from you loan officer, call them and ask them to help you decipher the report. You might even be able to get them to put an 'X' next to anything on your report that they think is hurting your profile. Since you don't want to dispute anything that is helping your profile, this will give you a good place to start deciding what you are going to dispute in your Credit Repair letters. You can dispute collections, charge offs, public records, bad debts. As I stated previously, if you have had a bankruptcy, you probably have a lot of accounts on your report that still show balances when they should not since they were included in your bankruptcy. Start with these.

Now that you know what you want to dispute, you need to write credit dispute letters. This is basically what a credit repair company would do for you, but you can do it on your own pretty easily. There is software available on the web that you can purchase and there are free sites that you can use. You should seek these out if you would like to save yourself a lot of time. If you have a lot of time on your hands (who does?) you can write the credit repair letters out yourself.

Sending out basic credit dispute letters is typically very effective, especially if the letters really look like they are from you and not created by a program. Some software will actually help you do that. You don't want the text and font to be the same on all the letters. Change it up a bit.

From personal experience helping people send out basic credit dispute letters, I can attest that they can be very effective in getting your report to be more accurate, and in improving your credit score tremendously.

What Everyone With Bad Credit Should Know About Credit Repair Services

If you're one of the millions of people in America with bad or damaged credit, don't despair. There are several things you can do to improve your credit. If you're looking for information about how to repair your credit and credit repair services, you've come to the right place. In this article we'll discuss the definition of bad credit and the benefits of using credit repair services. By the end of this article you should be able to start repairing your credit today, whether you choose to do so on your own, or hire a professional service to assist you.

What is Considered Bad Credit?

Most lenders define bad credit as any credit score lower than 620. After the subprime mortgage fiasco, some lenders are even raising that bar to 640. In addition to your payment patterns and amount of outstanding debt, your time on the job and your time living at your current address make up a portion of your creditworthiness. People who stay at the same employer and residence longer are considered more creditworthy than those who change jobs or move frequently.

If you are interested in improving your credit, it's in your best interest to know what your credit score is, even if you are afraid to find out! Order a copy of your credit report and make sure you get reports from all three major credit reporting agencies: Equifax, Experian and Transunion. Some lenders use the top score and some use a blended score so it is important to know what is on each report. Once you know where you stand you can begin the process of repairing your credit.

Benefits of Credit Repair Services

Credit repair services can help in a number of ways. Many of them offer packages that include obtaining your credit report, looking for inaccuracies and contacting the reporting agencies on your behalf. The primary benefit of credit repair services is that they save you time and effort. Most of what a credit repair service can do, you can do for yourself. But just like many services, the benefit is in convenience and saving time. It's akin to repairing your own car; it is technically possible for you to do it yourself, but if you lack knowledge and experience in repairing cars, you could probably save a lot of time and frustration by paying someone else to do it for you.

There are credit repair service companies that do not offer a true value because they use ineffective and/or outdated tactics. Some of the large and well-known companies are guilty of this. Make sure you investigate the credit repair service that you're considering and find out exactly what they offer. Get all of their claims in writing and find out what their refund policy is. Do not pay any fees up front (with the exception of a one-time set-up fee), and when in doubt, walk away.

Credit problems can be difficult to deal with, but help is available. The first step is determining your credit score and looking at the contents of your credit reports. Then decide if you want to take on the task of disputing negative listings yourself, or if you want to bring in a professional credit repair service to help. Credit repair services can save you time and effort although they can't really do anything for you that you couldn't do for yourself. When shopping for a credit repair service, make sure you investigate them thoroughly to protect yourself from any scams. With the information in this article you should be better informed about the best way to repair your credit.

Improve Your Credit Score - Credit Repair Companies Put To The Test

As a consumer credit advocate, I get asked all the time can credit repair companies improve your credit score?

The simple fact is yes! You can improve your credit score and get pre-approved for credit cards and prime rate loans by hiring a reputable credit repair company to work as your advocate. There are many companies that advertise credit repair services, but asking the right questions will help you decide which company is the most reputable and the best fit for your goals. With the best credit repair company on your side, collecting the facts will help you improve your credit score.

In order to improve your credit score, I suggest you ask the following questions before hiring a credit repair company:

• Do they have a Better Business Bureau record? Legitimate and reputable companies maintain a satisfactory record with the Better Business Bureau (BBB). Accredited businesses are committed to its customers and maintain the highest standards of trust and reliability. Visit bbb.org to verify satisfactory rankings of the credit repair companies you are considering.

- Is the company a law firm? Attorneys are bound by rules of ethics that require them to act with absolute integrity. Attorneys are responsible for looking after their clients' best interest and are required to utilize custom approaches to call upon every means possible to obtain positive results for their clients. Most companies, law firms or not, charge around $39 per month, so you should demand representation from a law firm for the same price to improve your credit score.

- Is a free consultation available? You should be able to discuss your goals and expectations before you enter into a contract with any credit repair company. You should also be advised of your rights under The Fair Credit Reporting Act (FCRA) [http://www.825credit.com/fcra.html] and learn how the law is on your side to help you improve your credit score.

• Can you cancel at anytime? Hiring the right credit repair company to represent you can help you gain better credit and improve your credit score. As results are obtained, you will not require the services of a credit repair company forever. Once you improve your credit score, reputable credit repair companies will allow you to cancel your account.

• Are online account management tools available? Reputable credit repair companies allow you, the client, to choose how you want your case managed to improve your credit score. Good credit repair law firms will give you options and advice on how to achieve the best results and will allow you to manage your case via a secure online client website.

• How many items have they removed for their clients? Legitimate credit repair companies have a proven track record of success. Companies such as Lexington Law have helped over 400,000 clients delete millions of items that are serious enough to harm your access to credit, prime loan rates and even a job.

I understand the challenges that you've encountered on your quest for better credit and, more importantly, a better life. You've been climbing a mountain; the right credit repair company can help you reach the top.

Fixing Your Finances With Credit Repair

If you do not think credit repair can help you out there are some things you need to consider. First of all how did you get into financial trouble? Did you lose your job? Did the monthly expenses overtake the monthly income? Did you make some bad investments? Whatever the reason there is something you can do to help and this rebuild. It will not be fun, it will not be easy, it will not be quick, but you do have to do it. If you are in financial trouble because you lost your job or you still have it but are trying to find a new one with no luck there may be something working against you. Let's say you find a job that pays well, has great benefits, and it fits everything you want. Well there are probably at least one hundred people who would be in the same situation as you are and they want that job too. Now if you all have similar qualifications; college degree, years of experience and so on, what is to separate you from the other one? More important, what will make you stick out when they are looking at you as an employee?

Shockingly the answer is your credit score. Many companies, in fact over forty percent of the companies around the country, have been using a credit check as part of their application process for years. This has been going on for decades and companies use it to thin the list of qualified applicants. It mainly happens with jobs that have certain financial responsibilities but that can cover so many jobs these days. Even companies feel it is a bit unfair but they cannot find another way to fairly choose between qualified applicants. So this becomes the most common method to help them make a decision and if you have been struggling with bills lately, you are going to be in trouble.

There are other things that can be hurt if you have a low score. Your ability to get loans, financing options and the interest you will have to pay when you borrow money. It really seems unfair that because your number is low you have to pay more a month on money owed. However, there is something you can do about it. Fixing your score with traditional methods takes too long to help you save money now. The only way to really save money is if you use credit repair now. By using the methods of credit repair to fix your score you will be able to reduce monthly payments with loan and credit companies. If they do not agree to adjust the deal and you have a good score you can transfer to another lender who will be happy to take you.

Section 609 Credit Repair Method

To understand how the FCRA Section 609 credit repair method works, it is important to understand that the FCRA was written before the advent of the internet. As such, they require the credit reporting agencies to have physical copies of all documentation to support each account that is being reported on. This is a problem for these agencies as virtually all credit items added to your credit report these days are submitted electronically. This in turn, means that it is rare for any documents to be reviewed prior to changes being made to your credit report.

Essentially, the credit reporting agencies just give all creditors the benefit of the doubt when new information IS added to your file. You can use this to your advantage by asking for hard-copy verification via Section 609 of the FCRA for virtually anything negative that is listed on your credit report. You simply need to use the following letter and not be deterred by any scare tactics that the credit reporting agencies will use to cover their tracks as they will try everything in their power to avoid having to tell you that they do n't have the physical documentation.

There are many sections and subsections in the Fair Credit Reporting Act that was established in 1971. Remember that the FCRA was established to protect the consumer from unfair lending and collections practices. One such section that can help the consumer dispute debt and information contained in their credit report is Section 609.

How does Section 609 help you repair your credit?

Section 609 of the Fair Credit Reporting Act says that upon a consumer's request, the credit reporting agency must be able to provide certain information to the consumer.

What this means is that you legally have options to get the credit reporting agencies to verify the debt on your account. I went into an explanation of the verification of debt in the last blog post so you should understand it a little bit. Like we talked about, a lot of the information on your credit report may be inaccurate.

Some of it may be accurate. It's important to make sure that the debt on your credit report and all the information contained therein is accurate. The credit reporting agency must be able to prove that the account listed belongs to you, and also where they received this information regarding this account.

The legal wording in Section 609 of the FCRA doesn't have information pertaining to whether the negative account is valid or not. What the law does care about is that the information the credit reporting agencies have on you and the accounts listed in your report is enough to provide proper verification under the law.

When you send a verification letter to the agencies, you are sending a request under Section 609 of the FCRA. You will be asking that the credit reporting agencies follow the law and verify the debt as requested. The credit reporting agencies have 30 days from receiving this letter to go through the verification process and get back to you. Make sure you keep foolproof records of everything you do through this process.

When you mail the 609 letters to the credit reporting agencies, send them certified mail with return receipt. This will cost you a little bit of money on the front end, but it will be worth it to have peace of mind in your record keeping. When mailing them certified, you will be able to track them and see when they are received. If the credit reporting agency does not respond to your dispute request within 30 days of that date, they are in violation of the law and you can call them out on it.

If they fail to respond to your 609 letters within 30 days, you can request that the credit reporting agency removes the disputed items from your credit report since they neglected to follow the law.

Your letter may be classified as "frivolous" by the credit reporting agency. The reason this happens is that they use computers to scan the incoming letters and classify them into categories. It would be rare for an incoming letter to go directly into a human's hands first thing. The credit reporting agency will then respond to your inquiry letting you know that it thinks your request is frivolous. You will have to send a second round of 609 letters.

To avoid having to do this process multiple times, you can put it a little more work on the front end, ensuring that a human will handle your dispute request instead of a computer.

When making the 609 letters to send to the credit reporting agencies, do not use an internet form letter. I will later give you examples of letters you can send but do not use them word for word. Instead, use them as a template or a guideline for what you will send.

Also, do not type your letter up in a word processing program like Microsoft Word or Google Docs. Instead, write your letter out by hand. Use blue ink, since it is harder for the computers to decipher. Write in print rather than cursive, as we want the human that looks over your information to be able to clearly read what you are asking of them. It is also a good idea to get the letters notarized before you mail them. This will prove to the credit companies that you are who you say you are.

Responses

When the credit reporting agency responds to your dispute request, they will do so by mail. There are a few different ways they can respond.

One way is a full and complete verification of your debt, like a copy of the original dated contract bearing your signature. If this is the response you get, the debt has legally been verified and you will be hard pressed to get them to remove it from your report.

Another way they try to verify the debt is not a true verification at all. The credit reporting agency may send you a copy of a statement on the line of credit that they received as proof from the original furnisher of the loan, or from a collection agency collecting the debt for the original lender. This is not solid proof of your debt. You will need to send another letter, requesting to see the copy of the original dated contract that has your signature on it.

The ideal outcome is that they credit reporting agency has no way to verify the debt in compliance with the law, and when they respond to you they tell you that. If this is the response, they need to delete the credit line off of your credit report. When the negative information is deleted, your credit score will improve.

After Dispute, Is it Gone for Good?

This is where some people get hung up. You are disputing your credit lines with the credit reporting agencies, usually not the person or company reporting the information to the agency. Unfortunately, sometimes even if the credit reporting agency deletes the inaccurate information from your credit report, it can come back to haunt you. If the original furnisher of the debt sees that the information has been knocked off, they may try to get it reinstated. They could also sell it to a collections agency which would start the process of verification and 609 letters all over.

If your debt was already with a collections agency when you disputed it and had it removed from your credit report, they won't be happy either. They could also try to get it put back on your report, or they might even sell it to yet another collections agency. Once again, this would restart the whole process of verification/609 letters.

Another thing you need to understand is that just because the debt is no longer reported on your credit report, that does not mean you no longer owe it if it is a valid debt. Make note of the fact that I said valid debt. If the information concerning the debt is invalid and you can prove it, you should have nothing to worry about during the dispute process.

However, if the debt is valid and you are just trying to get the negative reporting on the debt removed from your credit report; this process does not absolve you from paying that debt.

The 609 letters you sent to the credit reporting agencies were not sent to dispute whether the debt is valid or not. The purpose of the 609 letters you sent was to force the credit reporting agency's hand into proving to you that they have the legal right to report the disputed debt. If the credit reporting agency is unable to provide you with physical proof of the verification of the debt, they cannot report it on your credit report as they have no way to prove it is 100 percent accurate. The FCRA demands that the credit reporting agencies ensure that everything reported by them is factual, and this is where you have them most of the time.

Again, I will say if the debt actually belongs to you and the only reason you are disputing it is that of negative reporting, you still owe the debt. If you do not pay up on the debt, it will soon be sold to a collections agency, and then guess what? You will be right back in this situation again. Requesting that the credit reporting agencies verify that the information being reported by the collections agency is correct. If you are not careful and do not pay! attention, this an quickly turn into a vicious repeating cycle.

With the following "609 letters", you will need to be sure to always include a copy of a photo identification as well as a copy of your social security card (also include your past residences for 5 years). This is due to the fact that the FCRA only requires the credit reporting agencies to respond to individuals in writing if they provide these details. Without it, your letters will simply be ignored. When disputing accounts, it is also important to never dispute more than 22 at one time. This is the magic number, anything more than that will cause you dispute to be considered frivolous. Additionally, you will want to ensure you hand label your envelopes as type envelopes will be opened far less often.

Section 609 Dispute Letter Template

Name

Address

(Credit Bureau Name)

Date

To Whom It May Concern:

This letter is a formal complaint that you are reporting inaccurate and incomplete credit information. I am distressed that you have included the below information in my credit profile and have failed to maintain reasonable procedures in your operations to assure maximum possible accuracy in the credit reports you publish.

Credit reporting laws ensure that bureaus report only 100% accurate credit information. Every step must be taken to assure the information reported is completely accurate and correct. The following information therefore needs to be re-investigated. I respectfully request to be provided proof that these inquiries were in fact authorized With an instrument bearing my signature, and for legitimate business purposes. Failing that the unauthorized inquiry must be deleted from the report as soon as possible:

(Accounts you wish to have removed from your report)

Please delete this misleading information, and supply a corrected credit profile to all creditors who have received a copy within the last 6 months or the last 2 years for employment purposes.

Additionally, please provide the name, address, and telephone number of each credit grantor or other subscriber.

Under federal law, you have 30 days to complete your re- investigation. Be advised that the description of the procedure used to determine the accuracy and completeness of the information is hereby requested as well, to be provided within 15 days of the completion of your re- investigation.

Sincerely,

(Signature)

Name

SSN#

I will be providing you with templates for the letters we discussed previously. In case you skipped over those blog post to get to the good stuff, I will give a brief explanation again here.

You can send a Section 609/Method of Verification Letter forcing the credit reporting agencies to verify that they have proof of your debt from the original lender.

You can send a goodwill letter, asking for compassion regarding late or missed payments on a line of credit.

You can send a letter asking a creditor for a Pay-to-Delete deal to remove information from your credit report.

You can send an HIPAA letter for information regarding healthcare accounts on your credit report.

Remember, do not copy these letters word for word. They are just templates to give you an idea as to how to word your letters that you send. Do not print these, instead, write them out by hand. Consider having them notarized to further prove your identity to the credit reporting agency. Send the letters by certified mail only, with a read receipt.

Along with the dispute letters, you will need to send information proving who you are. Write another document and include the following information:

Your full name. This includes your middle initial and any suffix such a Junior or III

The date you were born

Social Security Number (if you have one)

Current and former addresses from the past 5 years

A copy of a government-issued photo identification, such as a driver's license

Copy of bank statement, utility bill, insurance statement, etc. to verify your current address and identity

Sample Letter 1

[Date]

Credit Reporting Agency/Bureau

City, State, Zip

To Whom It May Concern:

I have reviewed a copy of my credit report and am writing to dispute some information that needs to be deleted from the report. These items should be deleted for the following reasons:

Item #

Reason for Deletion

According to the provisions for consumers provided in the Fair Credit Reporting Act 611(a) [15 USC 168ii(a)], these items I am disputing must be re-investigated or deleted from my credit record within 30 days. While the investigation is ongoing, these disputed items must be removed from reporting on my credit report, or listed as "in dispute". I am also requesting the contact information of the individuals you communicated with during your investigation into this dispute.

When the investigation is complete, please notify me that the above items have been deleted in accordance with 611 (a)(6) [15 USC (a) (6)]. Please also furnish me with an updated copy of my credit report, to be sent to the address below. According to 612 [15 USC 168ij], I should pay nothing for this report.

If you need additional information or have any questions regarding this dispute, please contact me at address noted below.

Thank you.

Sincerely,

YOUR NAME

Address

City, State, Zip

Social Security #

Using Section 609 of the FCRA to Restore NOT Repair Credit

A simple, relatively unknown but proven legal strategy can be implemented to raise FICO scores 60 to 120 points. In 1999, H. Bruce McInnis Jr. in Maine looked at Section 609 of the Fair Credit Reporting Act (FCRA) and noticed something that, to his knowledge, nobody had ever noticed before; 609(c) (2) (E): "A consumer reporting agency is not required to remove accurate derogatory information from a consumer's file, unless the information is outdated under section 605 or cannot be verified."

If accurate derogatory information in the consumer's file cannot be verified, the reporting agency is required to remove it. This law requires every company that reports credit events, not just the original creditor companies, to be able to produce verifiable proof of the negative event. It holds the credit reporting agencies accountable for the negative information they pass on. This is obviously related to the right of debtors to challenge the accuracy of negative events reported on them. The intent of the government was to protect debtors from having inaccurate information used against them. The burden of proof is not entirely on the original creditors. All parties reporting this data are responsible for its accuracy. The companies that report credit events, besides the original creditors, are the credit bureaus; principally Experian, Equifax and TransUnion. Did they maintain verifiable records of people's debts? Mr. McInnis started challenging the credit bureaus to verify the negative credit events in the credit reports of his clients by producing a copy of the Original Creditor's Documentation. He did not challenge the accuracy of these events, just used a legal strategy to challenge the credit bureaus ability to verify their accuracy. In effect, he used Section 609 of the law to demand the credit bureaus justify their reporting. If they couldn't verify the data, they had no right to continue to maintain it on their credit reports. The credit bureaus began to comply. They removed the negative events from the credit records.

The credit reporting agencies don't maintain original document records of credit applications and events. They don't have a signature on a Visa card application. They don't have a signature on a car loan application. They don't have a signature on a bankruptcy filing. All they have are electronic blips in their databases. They simply accept what the creditors have reported to them about debtors. Even though the debtor knows it's accurate, the credit bureaus do not. They can't verify the accuracy of a single piece of data in their database. The credit bureaus are regulated by the government due to the nature of their business, but it's important to understand they are private companies. They are not legally or morally obligated to report anything on anyone. For example, most people know that most negative events remain on a credit report for seven years (ten years for Chapter 7 bankruptcies). This is not a legal requirement. In fact, they could take all bankruptcies off all records tomorrow, if they chose to. They are simply not allowed by law to report these events for more than seven years (or ten). They're not forced to report them at all.

Of course, it's their business. That's why they do it. But they have a choice and when forced to verify the data they report they will choose to take negative events off. Essentially, credit restoration doesn't eliminate negative credit events. It does make them in effect "invisible" to anyone looking at a credit report and this of course is reflected in the credit score.

Chapter Four

Credit Repair After Foreclosure

What a time to talk about foreclosures! It has been the top news at all the leading news agencies for some time and Americans are now experiencing the aftermath of a global crisis. What about the victims of foreclosure? What happens to their credit records? Everyone knows that the recent trend of foreclosures was caused by the economic crisis that affects the entire country, but unfortunately that won't be reflected in your credit report; the credit bureaus never consider 'why' the foreclosure took place.

Repairing credit after a foreclosure is a painful and draining experience. Credit repair needs to be done properly; otherwise, there will be a definite negative impact on all your financial activities in the future. As an example, you might not be eligible for a home mortgage or will have to pay a higher interest even if you do become eligible. Credit repair is a complicated but important process; you need to work on the matter with a lot of determination and consistency. There are three primary things you can do to repair your credit repair after a foreclosure:

- Pay your bills on time.
- Get professional help.
- Establish a budget.

Make sure that you keep track of your payment due dates and that you make your payments before the due date arrives.

Because of the possible complications, you may also want to get professional help for repairing your credit. If you find the right party to help you, this is a guaranteed way to get your credit repaired fast. Without help, you may end up in deeper trouble than what you are already in. Budgeting has also proven its effectiveness in repairing bad credit. You should establish a reasonable budget based on your income and liabilities and stick to it.

You can benefit from credit repair after foreclosure and get the credit rating you want and deserve to secure your financial future.

Fast Credit Repair - How To Raise Your Credit Score In 30 Days

If you are planning to apply for a loan, it would be a good idea to check your credit score and review your credit report. Lenders base their decisions regarding your creditworthiness on your credit score. This being so, you need to ensure that your score is based on accurate information. By taking some simple steps, you stand to raise your credit score in as little as 30 days.

Go over all the negative information on your credit report. The negative items would fall under any of the following categories: Repossession; Foreclosure; Write-off; Charge-off; Settled; Included in bankruptcy; Collection amounts; Court accounts such as liens, judgments, divorce, bankruptcy chapters 11, 7, or 13; Late payments; Inquiries.

Highlight any negative information that you know are inaccurate or misleading.

Some common errors include duplicate charges, accounts that belong to another person, or wrong balances.

Write a dispute letter to the credit bureaus concerning the inaccurate information. You have to identify the specific erroneous information, the reason why you believe the information is inaccurate, and what you want the credit bureau to do regarding the error. You may, for instance, ask them to delete or correct the error on your credit report. You need to enclose copies of documentation supporting your dispute, as well as a copy of your credit report with the highlighted inaccurate information.

The credit bureaus are legally obligated to investigate your dispute within 30 days. So, then, you may expect a response from them regarding the matter within that time frame as long as you have clearly communicated the necessary information and provided them with the documentation supporting your dispute.

Aside from taking steps to correct inaccurate information on your credit reports, there are other steps you can take that can improve your credit score within a month's time. One of the things that affect the calculation of your credit score is your debt to credit ratio, that is, the total amount of your debts divided by your total credit limits. If you pay off some of your credit card balances, you would lower your credit utilization ratio. The ideal ratio is just about a third of your total credit limit. Knowing this, avoid using up your entire credit limit. The restraint you demonstrate in your purchases would give a substantial boost to your credit score.

Exactly How to Rebuild Credit After Bankruptcy

When contemplating bankruptcy vs debt settlement it can really seem like a daunting task. But if the decision is made to declare yourself bankrupt then you should be ready to begin putting life back together after this difficult experience. In fact, many people just give up altogether and except a new lower standard of living. This should not be, it is not impossible to rebuild credit after bankruptcy, and much of it can actually be done relatively quickly if a strong plan is put into place.

First one needs to secure shelter after declaring bankruptcy. Renting after bankruptcy can sometimes be a hard task because many land lords require a credit check in order to lease property. One can usually overcome this problem by providing a little extra for a security deposit. By renting this way, one will rebuild credit after bankruptcy as well as secure shelter.

After an individual has a place to live they can then focus on other areas of rebuilding their credit. This can be done by contacting a credit services center. Because of the rising number of bankruptcies that are taking place nowadays professional credit service centers are being made available to help people get on with life and rebuild credit after bankruptcy. These credit centers have can provide useful information to people about how to make the bankruptcy experience less painful as well as how to get personal finances structured in a way that gives them a greater amount of leverage at building their new credit score up.

One technique that can be utilized is to apply for a secured credit card at a local bank. This is a credit card that requires money be put on it first before it can be used. It is similar to a checking account debit card, except that it is tracked by the bank and credit bureaus. Once an individual has established a responsible spending record with this secured card they will be able to have a low balance traditional credit card. This traditional credit card will allow one to rebuild credit after bankruptcy even faster, quickly leaving behind old worries of bankruptcy.

Conclusion

Anyone facing high interest rate loans or increasing rates on their credit cards would benefit from credit repair help. But, knowing where to go and how to employ solid credit repair help can be difficult to track down.

In reality, a lot of people offer credit repair help, but few deliver. The best means for obtaining credit repair help is to make sure you understand your own situation and some good common sense tenants for repairing credit first. If you do understand these things, finding credit repair help will be a snap because you will be able to discern who can help and who can't.

Finding solid credit repair help is a matter of understanding what you need to do to repair your credit. Whether it's paying off high interest rate loans and establishing a better debt to income ratio or erasing errors from your credit reports, knowing these things will guide you in your search for credit repair help. You don't have to be an expert at it, but a basic understanding is important. Leave the expert advice up to the experts if you're looking for credit repair help.

Let's take a look at a few scenarios where credit repair help could come in handy.

Bad credit

Credit repair help in this case might involve the need for a credit counselor to guide you on the path to fixing errors from the past. A person, company or even credit repair help computer program can assist you in targeting reasonable things you can do to improve your scores and pay down debts along the way. It is also possible the best credit repair help you can find in this situation is a consolidation loan to enable the closing of some accounts and the creation of a single, more manageable payment. If you can swing it and your debts are high, this is not a bad route to consider for credit repair help.

Errors

If you need credit repair help to fix falsehoods in your credit report, you will find a lot of assistance out there. There are people, companies and programs that all deal with credit repair help and that can help remove and dispute errors in recording on credit reports. It's also possible the only credit repair help you need is a willingness to dispute the issues yourself. Look into the process and see which route is the best option for you.

While credit repair help will vary in its scope from person to person and case to case, there is good help to be had. Just make sure you have a basic understanding of your own situation and some ideas on how to fix it first. Then turn to the experts for credit repair help if necessary.

Books by the same Author:

 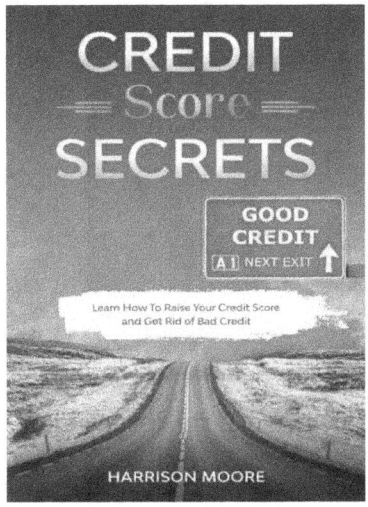

Search: "Harrison Moore"

at Amazon

Kind reader,

Thank you very much, I hope you enjoyed the book.

Can I ask you a big favor?

I would be grateful if you would please take a few minutes to leave me a gold star on Amazon.

Thank you again for your support.

Harrison Moore

www.ingramcontent.com/pod-product-compliance
Lightning Source LLC
Chambersburg PA
CBHW071407210526
45465CB00001B/285